Some of the Things I've Seen

By the same author:

Some of the Things I've Seen
Sara Berkeley

WAKE FOREST UNIVERSITY PRESS

First North American edition

First published as *The Last Cold Day* in Ireland in 2022
by The Gallery Press and edited by Peter Fallon

For permission, write to:
Wake Forest University Press
Post Office Box 7333
Winston-Salem, NC 27109
wfupress.wfu.edu
wfupress@wfu.edu

ISBN 978-1-943667-05-5 (paperback)
LCCN 2022948335

Designed and typeset by Peter Barnfather

Cover photo: "Fox in headlights" from *Fox About Town*
by Martin Usborne, courtesy of Lee Marks Fine Art, IN

Publication of this book was made possible by
generous support from the Boyle Family Fund

for George

Contents

Okjökull

"A plaque memorializing Okjökull, the first
Icelandic glacier lost to climate change, will
be installed next month."
— CNN, July 23, 2019

The ice sings beneath the glacier's weight.
I wake at five and there's no going back
to the dream state, only forward
through the tall gates of the day.
The past piles up, the memories of fires
send up their smoky prayers;
I cannot make them stop.

We need rain
to drown out the threat of burn.
The hills beneath their tinder beards
are blanched white brown—burned up
we call it, though there are no flames.
It's a slow burn
that has been going down
for decades now; I'm trying
to understand what keeps us safe,
what stands between us and harm.
The ice sings its long last song,
a requiem. Nothing
between us and harm.

In the amped-up nights
they come for me from the shadows
with their long knives.
I ride out before the dawn
to open wide the gates of my life.
I ride through the open gates
and the dark that kept me sharp
is still alive, it speaks to me
in tongues, but I feel it getting thinner
and the singing running drier.
Okjökull has drowned
beneath the weight of our desires,
our failures of resolve, of courage,
and our deafness to a calling that goes higher
and higher till the ice melts to fire.

Eight O'Clock Howl

Shifting colors. Sea changes.
Newness. Terribleness. Wonder.
Our world in the darkness made of glass
that's being stretched.

Birds. More than before. They perch
on the tips of trees I can see.
They know we've largely disappeared,
but they are about their business—
songs to bring on the dawn.
The dawns keep coming on,
louder than before, lovelier.

And the dusks, lonely with howling,
filled with voices, emptied
of all things but longing, despair,
thrill of connection, grief, loss, desire,
resilience, anger, determination,
hope, fear.

Kincade Fire

How little we know of any hour beyond this hour,
the backdrop to everything is joy,
the backdrop to everything is horror.
Wind shakes the redwood rain free of the trees,
a natural stripping down of the leaves,
a natural catastrophic fanning of the flames.
There is no limit to the elements of art:
lead earth oil straw seeds
etched polished glass paper pins hand wrought
copper gold paint, these are the things
we wrap around ourselves when we are hurt,
the backdrop to everything is love,
the backdrop to everything is fear,
three color sugar lift and photogravure,
everything we'll ever need is here,
steel plaster wedding dress razor wire,
how little we know of any hour beyond this hour,
the absolution of every forest is fire.

Podere Sette Piagge

I want to be here in the late afternoon
when the warm wind comes up
blowing the olive trees
till the undersides of their leaves
show more silver than green
and the fragile butterflies are blown
so they tumble round the lavender
and the white hydrangea.
What is this wind's name?
I need to stay here one more day
to learn the wind's name
and to slowly climb, when it dies down,
up to the city walls
and along the escarpment
to the Piazza del Popolo
where all the people are.

Solitude does not taste the same
as it used to. Yes, there is always
that room that memory stumbles into,
that bruised place with its ice knife
turning in time till memory blunders on,
enters another room. But being alone
is easier than it has ever been,
its simplicity washes over me
with all the names of Italian winds—
Bora, Ostro, Libeccio, Sirocco, Mistral.

Sharkbait

Contrary to popular opinion,
against all moods and expectations,
and although it was nearly five in the afternoon
I swam on Stinson Beach.
I swam and swam and the ocean loved me up,
slapping, boiling round me like icy soup.
I dived into the creamy afterbirth of the waves,
into the roiling orange gold of the low sun
against all medical advice
and with full knowledge and disclosure
because at that moment it mattered
to be alone with the sea and the sea alone with me;
because I realized that for all the day's patina of noise,
the shrill calls of the gulls,
and the emails and phone calls
when I am truly alone
I turn to poetry and poetry turns to me,
we bow,
perform some complicated little handshake
not even we know how to replicate
and begin to tussle.

Cruising Altitude

Somewhere over the pitted brown landscape
in a tin cylinder, my heart
is doing its flying.

Propelled by curiosity and thirst
for language, for new words,
and lust for learning,
I am following the sun.
It's hard to keep up. I try
until I'm tired, then I let go.

Up here, every day is wiped clean
by the soft cloth of night
and out of every dawn, birds carve
the name of the day in song
for all they are worth.
I turn in my sleep, still flying,
till I dream myself awake
and everything starts over.

There's nobody out there,
I've been watching.
Beyond the bottle-end transom
of the plane, we have the fields
to ourselves; we roam,
buoyed by our hopes
and the cottony whites,
anchored at ankle and wrist
to a home that is always in flight
and thirty-three thousand feet up.

Morning Number One

I'm alone in our room.
It's raining, lovely dove grey,
the forecast is for accumulating sadness
over the latter part of the day.

Let me be done with the business of doing
and the work of love, let me go down
to the lake with a pen, some champagne,
climb to the loft above the straight yellow bales,
let me free myself from all incarceration.

The sky will keep giving and giving
in a rage of sunset,
the night will move up the mountain
towards a color no one can name
left over by the last of the sun and, at the lake,
I'll see a landscape that shouldn't be there,
the low water mark from a famished year.

Yellow moon will rise over wasteland,
illuminating nothing;
I will string lights around the dark
and I will say my few words into that same dark
because night is the only vessel that can hold them,

small as they are,
too big for the light,
coming out fully formed
quiet and right;

and after the moon lays its shadow
over the forest of firs and the scrub
I'll drive to the ocean,
walk along the sand where the mole crabs
tickle my feet beneath the broken surf,
I will make my promise into the waves,
the ocean as witness;

a promise
that will lead me to the dawn,
and this: morning number one,
where the boy soprano comes in,
grief of innocence,
single violin.

Northern Lights

February first, above the terraced hills
skylark climbs to that ancient place
in the towering blue skies—
Gin is singing that she thinks it's love
gets us through all our goodbyes;
I think that's true, but every time
I call on love to pull me through
another memory or two
I get surprised.

Sax comes in like red velvet,
layers of me are falling clear,
this is how we are torn down,
this is how our core selves reappear;
we must strike out from the gravelly shore,
nowhere near safe from drowning
but well aware
there is no room for us
on dry land anymore.

Winter is broken; it cannot be put back
together; small birds in the maples
are singing up the weather;
sax moves from dark red
to deepest blue, and I am singing too,
skylark song is in my bones,
a soundtrack for the good news
of where I am
and what I get to do.

I step into my frail canoe.
The sun is fierce in the face
of dark clouds;
the dead are circling—let them—
it's the living I can hear,
their laughter drifts across the water
from the shore; I can't make out
their voices anymore
but now I'm sure
it's love
that pulls us through to the other side
and it's longing that propels us to the edge of the world,
the end of the skies and, through all of our goodbyes,
to the pole where we behold
the solar wind catching in the earth's
magnetic strings and playing them
like fabulous
green and pink and violet playthings.

New Mexico 68

On the road to Santa Fe from Taos
the sky went slowly wild with dawn pinks
and blues. I felt loose in my life, rattled.

Orange rain in the far South,
the Rio Grande riding by on its own time
with its own secret set of expectations.

Some nights before we had driven out
beyond the last of the mobile homes
to the end of the road; the Milky Way

wrapped her cool scarf round the moon's throat;
coyotes yipped and yowled
and the mesa dogs joined them;

I stood by the car, cold, a little jarred
and I wished someone would hug me
but nobody did. I'm glad.

Every evening after that we headed
to the Guadalajara Bar and Grill
and in the parking lot among the flatbed trucks

we watched the sky unfold and unfold
and unfold, and it felt good
to know just why I was afraid;

that sometimes it takes driving out
to where there's no more road,
to listen to the dark, and pick apart

the winking plane lights from the satellites,
hum a lullaby if humming is all you can come by
and let it burn away, the surface layer,

the jewelry, till you are down to something
more raw, more elemental, to where fear
lies quietly side by side with sadness,

anger, joy, whatever else you need in life
just to get by, to get you on that road to Santa Fe
and the airport and the plane and the home alone.

Hanuman

The temple garden trembled in the clear
early morning rain, lush
with hollyhocks, cosmos, leggy and leaning
heavily into the day.
In the meditation room
I sank to my knees, I put all hurt
to one side, there was ease,
the minutes passed like liquid
over the rocky floor, my thoughts were
stones beneath the river, waiting.
At noon in the Taos Cow Café
I lost connection, so I shut down
my machine and I turned
in another direction: scissors,
paper, stone. Hand, pen, page,
the connections that are always wired,
regardless of wi-fi,
no password required.
Early evening in the Manby gorge
I lay in the river, the river didn't care
what brought me there,
it flowed on over me
washing my clothes, my hair,
moving my memories like river weed.
On her birthday in early June
my mother stayed eighty, she was
not going on this time, she stopped;

but my daughter, born the same day,
she's going on, without my mum,
on her journeys around the sun.
I put my hands under the river's stones
so as not to lose my hold
in the flow, so as to feel their weight
on my bones, and the rain
began again, one drop at a time.

Rudolph

Consider that it may not be
the most wonderful time of year;
consider that the night may not be holy,
but full of rage and fear, and promises
that this will never reoccur,
never be this loud again, never go this far.

We are round the other side
of our brightest star, the short days
start with jewels of frost and end
with tears, the icicle lights are strung
from fear to fear, and in between

Rudolph with your nose so bright
won't you guide our flight tonight,
the way is barred, the shadow tall,
our rage is huge, and we are small.

Let's Pack All Our Clothes

October's aflame, and my world too.
My world is on fire, snatches of panic
as the red trucks siren by, the yellows,
the orange haze and bursts of gold
exploding out of the funeral pyre.
Sun on dry leaves and the tinderish wind
wrestling their whispered secrets from them:
Let's pack all our clothes, they say,
let's enter another state
until our warm familiar lives
are deeply strange to us, until we barely
recognize our own reflections.

The leaves are falling now,
mere skeletons of their former selves.
I took my clothes off hangers and shelves
and out of drawers. I closed the door
of our home behind me for a final time;
my keys don't work there anymore.
I park my car in the gravel turnout
overlooking the saltmarsh and the wreck
of a boat near the tide line at China Camp
and I look out over the broken view
of my life. I came here in the dark
the night our marriage died.

I called out to the wolves
and the hunter moon and its entourage
of stars: *Oh strangers with kind hearts,*
circle your wagons around me now,
things that spark and flare up into light,
illuminate my way tonight. It's a long
road from this moment to the dawn
and the map of my future just got erased
and redrawn and erased and redrawn.
It's cold, and I'm booked into a hotel,
third floor, overlooking the parking lot,
toothbrush in a water glass.

Rings Off

My life is another country now.
There are unfamiliar tracks in the snow,
there are fields of grain that burn, there is frost
that rises into mist in the December sun.

When I jumped
I thought there would be broken bones, I thought
there would be severe weather on the way down.
I didn't step or fall, I launched, and instead
it seemed the air was all
that held me there in its open arms.
The reservoirs of the human heart sent up their candy-
striped flags, their bugle sounds, their red balloons.
As I came down I saw the light leave the town
and I saw the promise of light return in the pre-dawn,
all of that, the endless circular goings-on of the globe
and, at midnight, fireworks and a gunshot,
and I hit the ground,
and I ran.

My rings are off, they are in
the tiny silver box I set aside for them
and here come the twelve bands of light
all the way from ultraviolet to infrared
taking me from utter darkness
to this outsized pale star in the dark
illuminating the warm rooms of my house.

Looking back I see now
those are my tracks in the snow, this is my exotic
garden of cloud out beyond the shadow of doubt,
my eulogy to fear, my brave new year.

Grace

I swam from the shore to the sandy spit
and on the way I dreamed of drowning
but I swam through the fear;
I walked up on the shaly sand
and my life was waiting for me there;
I lit a fire, violent at its heart,
it burned with ease through the driftwood
I had piled up as a shelter from the dark.

We came from desert,
moved through perpetual rain
that liquified the parched hills
and brought them tumbling down
with houses, trees, power lines;
as fast as everything fell apart
the good green world poured out
her liquid heart into the flood

and when the power went out
and the batteries ran down
I learned to wrap both arms
around the life-raft of the dark,
I learned that it's about
not being swallowed by the night,
that it's about letting the night storm
on and on, till out of a blue dawn, grace;

a world washed clean and calm,
and look now! April comes sailing in,
creaming over the sandbars with her
wildflowers in jam jars and her sudden
fern forests taller than a man, no more
anguish in the night, she turns
cold love inside out till you
can scarcely bear the heat

and the doors that were being pushed shut;
the doors are opening now, each day
in its own way a preparation.
If what will survive of us is love
then I will open too, I will allow the white
froth of trees, the four falling notes
of the mourning dove and the high
white clouds to make me unafraid.

For we are round the brighter side
of the sun, every revolution takes us
further from the fall chill, the winter
wet and stripped. Space opens up,
there's room for promise and for hope,
and though my fear was clean, and meant
something, I get up every morning now
and I laugh as I shrug the wings on.

Hospice Nurse

When I show up for death
I take off my thousand pound weight

so I go in light
and I wait

there by the bedside
for death to look up.

There's family: a daughter,
a wife, a son flown in

from the East Coast
and death thinks this is all

so fine, he has the elixir
for the dying man

in his coat, in the pocket
of his heavy coat.

But I am the hospice nurse
and I have something too,

I have a comfort kit
for when death decides

to really come out with it,
the twenty-one gun salute,

the frothing
at the mouth.

After I lay down my cloak
for the dying man

and the son calls out "Dad!
Dad! It's me!"

it's not good
or bad

but he can't hear him,
he can't hear any of them

he is on his knees in the fine sand
staring out to sea.

Strangers' Doors

How is it
to knock on strangers' doors
and enter where you are called for?

It's still warm
in the rooms of the dying,
but I am cooled from inside.

Fear keeps me tall
and knowledge keeps me slow and still,
treading gently. The dying know more than I know.

Even the moments
that are nothing, that are emptied out,
have weight.

In the room with us,
Mozart's *Requiem*, as sung
in the Basilica of Saint-Denis,

the chorus
lifting the lid off the skies, violins
sending up their prayers, cellos *arioso*.

Outside the window
last year, clinging to the trees,
and the heavy bear coming down the slope.

The dying
are filled with the hours of their lives;
they are open, awake to themselves. Apart.

I stand witness
in the bethel of their suffering
and in the sanctuary of their ease.

Everything. Alright.

Late afternoon. Burger Hill. Fat light.
I just came from her house.
I bathed her. Dressed her in her favorite top.
Left all her rings, her bracelets,
her necklace around her slender neck.

I put all her medicines in a special bag.
Dotted the i's. Sat in my car a while
outside her place. Made a call.
Sat a while. Wiped my eyes.
Some deaths take us further than we realize.

I'd like to visit her again
tomorrow, ten a.m., as we planned.

She went out her own way.
Lipstick. Decked out nails.
In her last few days
she mouthed to us, *yeah,*
it's all going to be okay.

The air outside my car
is pale gold, busy with life,
flitting things, shiny spiderweb,
birdsong I can't identify.
I feel her.
I'm not sure
but I think she's telling me: Get on home.

Pick up your life, girl,
No sense hanging around for me,
I'm done here. Go be yourself.
This is a good life
and when the night is dark blue and black
and white, remember me
and how I whispered to you with my last breaths:
Everything. Alright.

Early Morning Call

I'm too tired tonight for the stories
of the dying, their needs
crowd me,
exhaust me. I know their needs
far exceed mine, or anyone's
in my life, but I am also
mother, daughter, wife.

Pull close
the people I have with me now,
wrap around a comforter
against the chill of night.

Patients
die right after I go off shift,
they die before dawn
and on the weekends,
times I can't be there
or do more.

Drive by the hospital,
drive by the graves.
This morning I dressed
for the last time
a man whose two young daughters
had made for him
a shirt that said: *World's Best Dad*,
and signed it on the back.

Alone in the room with him
I slipped it over his head
and pulled it down.
I felt that he was there,
that wherever he was,
he saw.

Rain or Shine

Late September,
thunder low in the night's throat,
four-fifths moon, restless trees,
first geese heading south.

The land's good bones are laid out
in patterns I have grown to love;
they tell me stories that become a part
of my story. The hills and hollows
are painted greens of rain or shine;
they turn my sadness.

Hot night. Under my single
sheet I stretch my body out.
Awake beneath the fan
I touch on each of my dying folk.
This one closer, this one not so close.
I promise into the dark
that I will try to keep them comfortable
so they won't die in pain.
That's all any of them really ask
in the end—someone to listen hard,
someone along with them
on the last stretch of road
until the stones run out
and the wind takes their breath.

Ghost

for Monica

School's out
kids mill at the bus
cars jam up the road
the parking lot clears.
Classrooms
lose their laughter
and the parents pull away.
But one car's not there
cos there's a ghost in the chair.

AP art is noisy
AP lit's intense
basketball court is jumping
pool's a water-polo world
Precalc test tomorrow
school flag gets unfurled
over the football field
mountain biking team sets off
for the ultimate downhill.
One bike's not there
cos there's a ghost in the chair.

Ghost sits in my house
rides shotgun in my car.
Ghost with red hair.
Every tall kid with a jaunty walk
reminds me. Ghost. Walked. There.
Once kissed my girl.
How come he's not here?
Defies all understanding
why there's a ghost in that chair.

Sometimes
when I tell my girl goodbye
I catch a glimpse of ghost
out of the corner of my eye.
And I wonder if his smile
is a trick of the light
or if he lingers here
to let us know,
me and her,
girl he thought so beautiful
on some ordinary day,
that it's all really, now and always,
going to be okay.

Wood Thrush

Where I turn at the long barn
it's still good. Beyond the creek
and Mill Hook, past the deserted summer camp
the road goes inward to a wary place,
somewhere damage was done.

My business is at the trailer park.
Outside their double-wide
bucket chairs, a fridge.
Bikes scattered on the rutted road.
Kids all inside.

My visit
bears witness
to generational pain.
I take it in by listening,
by feel, the suffering
finds a place in me.

I drive home through the flutter
of scintillate gold leaf, scatter
of chipmunk and squirrel;
an October so warm cicadas
still flex their tymbals.
Slowly over the miles
I empty out, and into my
hollowed-out self
pours a two-note song:
wood thrush, rise and fall
simultaneously sung.

Some of the things I've seen
still have a beat inside me:
suffering of the dying,
counterweight of trees aflame,
pull of tide by the moon,
sandhill cranes against dream.

Last Date

Snow finds me
in my own form of silence,
drift of words. Adds some layers,
grey blue two-note bird calls.

Roads white from salt,
creek running on in tea light,
whole of the day flowing by.

He called to his wife
from the other room.
She climbed in his hospital bed
with him.

We flicker like lights.
We go out like stars.

Just the one bird now
holding an impossibly high note
and the sorrowful comfort of trees.

Skin of Ice

All day I've been inhabiting my life
and my life inhabiting me,
vessel and conduit, barefoot
in the stream of it, until it gets too much,
too concentrated being this alive,
and I have to leave.

On the road to their house
skin of ice left on the ponds,
the last few grubby mounds
of snow, I'm thinking through
what to say.

The land around their house
is steeped in snow history,
fall after fall
blunting the prints,
and the whetted stones, the mistakes;
skin of snow
frail as the membrane between
the living and the dying.
I'll say it to her wife:
I believe she's dying,
no pause around the word
it's part of the day, the hour,
part of her room now
like furniture.

When I leave their house
the trees lean in close,
fall quiet as I pass.

Snow on Molesworth Street

A journey home, February's bitter end,
that hard-won piece of ground
on which I stand
proves a floe. Terminal Two,
walking on glass out into the chilled sun,
all the words aslant on my native tongue,
a brisk wind shivers across the puddles,
funny the things that right us.

Four days in Dublin, the heavy doors,
you have to put against them all your years
before they give, but when they give
they offer up their inner rooms without reserve:
Titian, Velazquez, Turner's sunset
at Ostend with its fiery skies,
and Christ taken before our eyes,
the hand of betrayal on his cloak
and the dark, the soldiers' darkness,
their intent.

Thirty-one years
and I'm always leaving Ireland,
its salt rime, black rocks, white caps,
the sea coming in at the land.
I travel from end to end,
the melancholy begs to be let in
but I drive her out into the weather,

sun, rain, sideways dance of sleet
and snow on Molesworth Street,
the spirits so light in weight
they forget to settle.

Terminal Two:
we taxi down the runway,
the roots that were nourished in this soil
are coming loose,
takeoff rips them free, the wrench

in the chest, the heart crossways
and salt rime, every time,
as the plane banks steeply over the Poolbeg twins
and the melancholy wails to be let in,
I use all the words I know—
bracken, bog, and fen, skeletal trees,
moss covered stone, and slowly
they are enough
for the ghosts to leave well alone
so in the end
I'm just as strong
as the hard-won piece of ground
on which I stand.

Luminous

Almost
hit a fox
on my way home.
He ran out
small
pale brown
bushy guy
zigzagging
in the headlights.
I swerved.
I was a
house on fire.
He didn't burn,
a flood,
he stayed dry.
He stayed alive
despite my
XJ8 killing machine.
I'm in my house now
and he's free,
running between trees,
by the stream,
awake
in his fantastic dream,

alive and free
in
spite
of
me.
He might even be
curled up small
breathing
evenly
dreaming
of the luminous
whites
of a human's eyes.

Palio

Three flights up
in the white heat of afternoon
he is sleeping off the wine.

This adventure,
they both drink to it,
could well be his last.

When he gets home
they will run tests,
send probes.

In his secret heart
he believes they'll find
what they are looking for:

mets to the bones,
the liver, the lungs,
he did all that drinking

and he feels he should pay;
she disagrees, but he tells her:
without fear

there would be no clarity
to the edges; without loneliness
and the threat of loss

no depth perception
only black and white
and riotous color

no sepia tones,
no yellows and browns
of mahogany, brocade,

and without the will to win
the ten wild horses
would keep stampeding

round Il Campo
in an endless, riderless,
frenzied Palio.

I Am Giving It To You Straight

Dreaming of you
grown younger
your hair longer
alone with me
in the hot bustle of this town;
wraith by my side
a work of smoke
and silhouette, ghost
in your slender human form
unusually pale even for you,
ethereal, your hand
on my arm your shirt
bright white, crisp,
your eyes too smoky
to read, smile
impenetrable so familiar
so strange as you recede
slowly to your distant place
aloof and cool now
suddenly ash grey
transparent, changing
as we walk
up the Via Guicciardini
past the shimmering Boboli
you are thin and loose
your limbs like bones
in their too-big clothes;

we reach the Analena
you are scarcely here
a chimera, *amici*,
a walking host of memories
but suddenly clear, in focus,
memory made whole
and laughing now:
around us, bells of noon
peal down from Santo Spirito
and wash the Oltrarno
with clean waves of sound.

Open Heart

for George

Seven hours in
the lungs are flat, pushed aside,
the muscles are cut, and the heart
is utterly hushed,
the stillness in the chambers chills,
and the quiet has a weight, a depth;
add to it a drumbeat,
a single horn, a violin,
let the boy soprano part begin
and the lush orchestra come in,
I cannot bear the silence.

Deeply unsafe to love like this,
out, far out on the limb.
Six years before I knew of him
he was laid out on the table
bared to the surgeon's blade.
Over his face a cotton mask,
hands and feet all painted black
so the clouds could recognize him,
and high above,
a hole in the dome of the sky
where swallow and shriek
could show the spirit a way out
should the spirit need to depart.

But this man's spirit was titanium strong
and it had already sung
a long and complicated song;
it hovered close to his heart,
on vigil, waiting out the hush,
and when the blood shuddered back
and the lungs fluttered and ballooned
it set up its kind of singing once again,
sweeter than before,
still untempered, rich with pain.

After Light

In the backs of our minds
before any of us can recall,
before the journey down the birth canal
deep memory's delicate trace
reminds us of the metalsmiths
who hammered out our souls
in the icy heat of the night,
molten metal flowing
through the network of sprues,
details cold worked and chased
as the wax was driven from the mold
and love was beaten
into the slip of the gold.

Down in the hungry depths
in the shadows thrown
on the lunar water
by the annular moon
the chatelaine rattles her keys,
keys that unlock the delicate birdcage
of the spine, and the long-buried songs
that the brain sings
from behind its bars,
songs of longing
for a still center and a solid core.

We cling so tightly
to the scaffold of our lives
until night loosens the hold.
We drift out
into the waters of the dark,
lie still in the ghostly waters
and let the caravels take us.

Blue Trees

The linen canvas on our bedroom wall
has a beating heart, rapid, neonatal.
Cobalt blue so far,
just blue branches.
I lean in close with my stethoscope
to establish the presence or absence
of vital signs.
So much for the death of painting.

At the angle of incidence,
in the yellow glow of the year's
second supermoon, more light
means more information.
I gather it: we could be twins
separated by sixteen years,
breakbulk reunited at last
on the long shore. I am writing you
this love poem with its taste
for blood and tears because I am tired
of all separation, because I'm casting around
for a foothold on the surface
of this slippery world
and you have promised we can be
just loose enough to slip through
all border crossings with our
quicksilver syllabary, just tight enough
to hang together on our paper raft
to survive the death of poetry
and the demise
by pandemic
of art.

Foxes

Up before light. In the clear
inky air outside the front door
a fox bark down near the creek.
Who could replicate?
Maybe a call to mother from child,
maybe distress or hunger,
or just the thrill of running
past water, past barn, past
human enclosure.

On our wedding cake
two foxes, turning in unison
toward the beacon fire of dawn.

Covid Migration

When I'm dead and gone my immortal home
will hold me in its bosom safe and cold.
— Jolie Holland, "Goodbye California"

Outside my door
the garden is too proud to beg for rain.
Seared California, burning with desire,
ash cloaked, feverish.
My phone says it's 1:44 but I don't know where.
I'm unmoored, unsure when any time begins
or ends, it's just now, and still now,
darkness released over the land.
What is that word for strengthened by fire?

We pack the car
in the dark. Four days' drive
as the swallow flies.
Basin and range. Sage and mormon tea.
Wyoming,
so much harsher than I thought it would be,
billboards for fireworks, Jesus, and guns,
and on the blue freeway signs
state after state's small towns
all bound by the same chains:
Subway, Arby's, Casey's General Store.
What kind of fear is at work here?

Each night
the same motel,
same carpet,
same ice machine.

We cross the Hudson
on the Newburgh–Beacon Bridge.
Sunday evening lays across the summer farms
and along the Taconic State Parkway.
Out of the ashes of our old life
rise these barn stars, the fields with horses,
and long green lawns drunk with rain;
a sudden right turn onto a dirt driveway
up a hill to our new home
that we have never seen.

In the caves at Lascaux
Magdalenian hunters with manganese
sketched a great black cow
escorted by horses on the apsidiole.
Horse 59 had seven spear wounds.
Horse 60 advanced, sniffing the ground.

We have torn ourselves out of our lives,
given up our ghosts and come
three thousand miles.
This place is gentle. Welcome
is what you make of it.
Tempered. That's the word.

Wind Advisory

They called a wind advisory,
an oxygen-dependent power shutoff
warning danger state of alarm.
I drove home
on brand new roads,
just beginning to learn,
just beginning to let go,
first glimmer of trust
in a landscape bright with fear,
wide open. Frighteningly so.
Leaves swirled around my car,
moves on the gleaming asphalt
so showy they made me laugh.
Unexpected. A start.

This storm—
they said it would cause harm
but the air outside my car,
the air I saw,
solid with light, scumbled with cloud,
seemed to promise me, newcomer,
it would stay warm, benign.
It looked like air I had seen
before. Back home.

They called a wind advisory,
I realized they meant
drifts of gold in the gutters.

Clinton Hollow

I live in a town that is hardly a town,
just a hollow, the road dips down
past the green town sign
to a creek; some houses,
some red barns, an old mill
with a wooden waterwheel,
bends in the road that lead
to accidents of light,
stillness resting on the ponds,
the riots of trees.

I'm afraid. My dreams bear this out.
I get up, it's late. I say to the night—
what are the names for the blues you use,
are they French and rare,
bleu Louise, bleu Céleste, bleu lumière,
or watery: sea blue, navy, aquamarine?
Night lets her intricate lace run down
the windowpane. There's
violet and some manganese,
a hint of white, of indigo,
some orange for a little mystery.
This is how it all works.

When the dawn comes round
I'm lying in wait. In the low brightness
she reveals white after white:
lilac, seashell, cool bice.
Birds begin to let their guard down,
they start to call, and the dawn
layers in antique ivory, whitesmoke,
all the colors of a wedding veil,
all the colors of a funeral pall.

It is too late
to try for sleep,
I put some coffee on.

Through the skeletal trees
a fox crosses Hollow Road;
towards the creek he hesitates
somewhere between violence and gentleness
and breaks open the porcelain morning.

In the Middle of Last Night

In the middle of last night
we were born, awake and alive.
Moon raced down the road
followed by plows.
I need snow boots, good gloves.
We live very close,
I watch you doing things,
I know every face.

I did not think ice would be this green.
Ponds freeze to a center hole
where I fall in. White sky bleaches out
over the bones.
My hands have gone on without me.

All night the plows drove back and forth.
Don't expect to get much done,
warns winter. *You need to spend time
adoring me.*

Turning Point

for Jessie

It wasn't the longest dark, solar midnight,
equidistant from dusk and dawn
when the aching stopped

and it wasn't the moment I buried winter's faint heart
in the freezing soil, patting it down,
hoping against hope

or the unknown, unmarked nanosecond
when our sun burned halfway through
her brief candle.

It was the giddy embrace
on the curb in the standing lane at JFK,
a moment that drew us both
into a thin sliver of time outside our lives.
The world around us, cold
and broken in her turning,
permitted us our burning
after five months apart, binary stars,
blue hot to our inner layers,
open to everything.

We drove east through the penitents.
Snowfields shone in the dark.
We raced the moon, forging our lives
from the available materials.
I felt a gravitational shift
from grief and loss and, in the passenger seat
my daughter, blazing under her own power,
took the dark and struck it
against the air, until the air
danced with streamers of light.

Dutchess 18

It's raining hard and loud,
the last hours of March. No longer
bone cold we've earned
our reward. We learned
how winter was put together
as we took her apart.
Each day hit its hammer just so,
twenty kinds of snow,
the stone walls froze and thawed
and, against the ice, each day
stretched out a little longer,
a little more luxurious
in the looseness of the right light.

We did this to ourselves,
drove away from the snug container
of our lives. A continent away
Pacific waves still crash against
the cliffs along the coastal highway
and climb up Muir and Limantour.
Over here the trees stand out
strong black against the blue
and grey blue and fugitive white
of the New England night.

Without a plumb line
our barn's tucked between
the swollen creek and the road,
Dutchess 18. We're sheetrocking
its century-old ceiling.
Gypsum and termite dust,
the ghost hands of those
who raised it. One day soon
it will be home to jars
of alizarin crimson, cadmium green,
rolls of cotton duck, linseed oil,
and an empty white painting wall.

Bird Room

It's that time of night,
blue-black between the trees.
A week since my daughter left, ten days,
the guest room hollowed out,
the bed remade.

April went off with a last shake,
wind and petal showers, May came in
already fat on colors: violet
lilac and the splash of trees
trying on their summer dresses,
crab apple pink fanfare, dogwood
blossoms bruised white at the edge.
I lie on the guest bed, the day
outside is delicate;
my heart finds room
to make sorrow matter, make it
mean something.

Overnight
the dandelions go to seed, the air
drifts.
No matter how much you love it,
how much you beg, spring moves on,
taking with her the young light
yellow and lime
on the early maple leaves.
In the bird room
sun glows on the honey wood floor.

Guest List

I need words that have not been invented yet,
now that we are woken by thunder,
footsteps on the water,
life with its insistent beat
will not let us hang back—today
we push on further than ever before,
making more of it, lightning
and a summer downpour,
at night we wheel and deal for another dawn
immaculate, one that the birds proclaim
before we are aware,
while the crickets climb the heat.
The horizon is broad brush strokes,
just an approximation, somebody's
best guess, nevertheless
we are making a guest list,
our coast-to-coast migrant souls
wide open to the gentle air, drift of cottonwood,
a pair of chords on the confident keyboard,
sweetness of pit fruits. After dusk
the stars ride up on their ferris wheels,
peonies bow down with the weight of loving,
and in the humpback dark, we turn over,
feel for each other's pulse.

Slow Fox Farm

One day the air smells cool,
you can feel it
sluicing out the dust of summer,
sounds like falling.

Slow Fox Farm: late afternoon.
A year since I first came here,
raw from our four-day drive,
in a place of wonder and bewilderment.

Everyone seemed to be coming together
and I was wandering loose
inside my cavernous life,
searching for landmarks.

You can stay where you are,
or you can move
as migrants move.

You can walk around
under the weight of living,
the loneliness and doubt:
but one day
the new roads look familiar,
you turn into your driveway
and you're home.

Through the sugar maples
September light is long and stretches out
to the four corners of the dark.

Monarchs

Sunset. After sunset. The barest glow.
Dawn after dawn rolls in
on the Miami shore's milky air.
That's not rain on the radar,
that's Monarchs
riding a cold front south.

I'm flying north,
forwards in time from tropical
to where the colors are starting
to sing themselves into being.
This morning I walked out in warm rain
with my daughter on the Keys.
Twenty years, three months, fourteen days.
Not that I'm counting.

Flight's delayed five hours,
storm in New York. Poor humans,
we are trying so hard,
but time is contracting, the future
keeps getting shorter. We barter.
It doesn't matter.

I'm watching a man with his sleeping son.
Dear honest, adoring dad,
I'm sorry about your baby's sold out dreams.
Thirty years will drown the Keys,
there is no money to raise the roads
or the grocery stores or the schools.
Hold on tight, hold on tighter,
the rafts they're sending
just keep getting lighter.

Monarchs' migrating wings
sound like waterfalls.
Three thousand miles
and five generations
sailing the hopeful winds
to Central Mexico
in the spring.

Ten to Six

Ten to six,
light is leaving the full belly of the creek
but before it leaves
it picks out the loose snow
thrown by the hand of the wind,
fires it in rose gold, amber gold and, finally
bronze. Then it is gone.
Without it the trees suffer and grow old,
the snow between the trees
turns blue with cold, wolves prowl,
the shapes of bears
cut themselves out of stone.

At dawn
it comes around again. Payne's grey
runs cool in the creek's veins
and across its liquid skin.
Geese at the water's edge feel it
shiver over their feathers,
and I watch it tune up the colors
of our waterlogged world.

I who was raised by ocean
and know in my bones the steely sea,
white caps and white dots of cottages,
thatches of vivid grass, dance of sun
and cloud, sun and cloud—
I am learning a new vernacular,
a land of ponds and streams,
pen and ink trees against the white air,
snatches of snow on a stone stair,
stone walls, red barns, and winter
moving from heavy
to middle weight
to feather light.

Milk Glass

After the ice storm,
the crackle and hiss of dirty weather,
the world encased in howlite stares out
at the sun and the sun
stares it down, painting on
a layer of glass.

It would be easy to lose heart
this far in, this cold weight of weather
getting steeper, more brilliant,
ice floes riding each other on the river,
tormented.

Rigor of winter.
Do not believe the silence you hear,
do not be fooled by the stillness.
Beneath the ice the blood runs.
Cold is a vessel for every kind of heat.
By the light of our one lamp
Mozart's *Requiem*
written between operas, between fevers,
fills the darkness beyond our thoughts,
the Kyries swell until
the small rooms we live in can barely hold it all,
burial service following Mass,
light through milk glass.

In our tight ship
where we go to sleep and where we wake up,
lying alive before the day decides,
I'm going to take tomorrow
and shape it with my bare hands,
copying the future out
letter by letter.

The Last Cold Day

Wake me, now I'm alive
and sensate, now I'm awake
on the last cold day
before snow's words
curl themselves back up
on winter's page.

Willows know it.
They were the first.
During the melt
in a landscape of monotones
they lit up slow
yellow gold, gilded,
throwing their bare arms
into the wild afternoons,
following age-old instructions
imprinted in the mother tongue
beneath the snow.

Geese know it,
a week of happy mornings
fattening by our creek.
I woke to their scandalous cries
and lay there loving them
immediately
and without reserve.

They have flown,
the creek runs on alone,
I lie beside you
before dawn
on the last chilly day
loving
completely
and without reserve.

Acknowledgments

Thanks to Peter Fallon and The Gallery Press, who first published this collection as *The Last Cold Day*. Thanks to Jefferson Holdridge and Alex Muller at Wake Forest University Press for their tireless encouragement and help with this edition.

Thanks to my family, especially my daughter Jessie and my dad for their enduring support. And to George, who never lets me forget that it all works out okay.